We're glad you've enjoyed
The Powerful You; the life-
changing international classic
enjoyed by millions.

This book can be purchased
at stores or ordered from
www.GodsChild.org/shop
and all online booksellers.

100%
Profits to
Charity

100% of all profits from the sale of this book are
used to care for, educate, and provide health
and home-building services to orphaned
children and abandoned women through
www.GodsChild.org. Check it out.

The
Powerful
You

¡Tú El Poderoso!

Written by
PATRICK ATKINSON

Illustrated by
ERNESTO ATKINSON

A Message for My Child
ISBN 13: 978-1-59298-605-7

Library of Congress Catalog Number: 2011939113
Printed in the United States of America

First Poster Printing: 1993
First Online Publication: 1995
Second Poster Printing: 1997
Third Poster Printing: 2002
First Book Printing: 2011
Reprinted: 2012, 2013, 2015, 2017, 2018
First Printing 2018: *The Powerful You*

Cover and interior design by StudioCollective.com
Illustrations © Ernesto Atkinson

StudioCollective.com   BeaversPondPress.com   HippoWallowPond.com

The Powerful You is available for purchase from AtkinsonCenter.org or your favorite retail or online bookseller. Wholesale, academic, religious, and institutional discounts are available. *The Powerful You / Message for My Child* by Patrick Atkinson is available for purchase in 13 languages worldwide.

For all growing people young and old

SPECIAL THANKS

In the journey of life, I've been one of the luckiest guys on earth and have worked with some of the finest people imaginable. To them, and for all who read my works, I say thank you. In particular for this book, I would like to thank the www.ITEMP.org teams for the amazing life-changing work you do to save thousands of lives around the world, Miguel Angel Alvarez Paz and Christopher Mathew for their patience and support through this and many other projects, Jon and Alyssa Thomas of Studio Collective for handling the lay-out concept and design, and Beaver's Pond Press, the publisher. My greatest thank you goes to my son and the illustrator of this book, Ernesto Atkinson, for whom the message in this book was finalized when he was a teenager.

This book has been entered into the Permanent Collection of the Art Institute of Chicago.

I can give you
life,
but I can't
live
it for you.

*Puedo darte una vida, pero no
puedo vivirla por ti.*

I can give you
instructions,
but I can't tell you
where to go.

❧

Puedo darte instrucciones, pero no puedo decirte a donde ir.

I can give you liberty, but I can't help you to protect it.

○

Puedo darte libertad, pero no puedo ayudarte a protegerla.

I can teach you
the difference between
good and bad,
but I can't make the
decision
for you.

*Puedo enseñarte la diferencia entre el bien
y el mal, pero no puedo decidir por ti.*

I can give you
advice,

Puedo darte consejos, pero no puedo aceptarlos por ti.

but I can't **accept**
it for you.

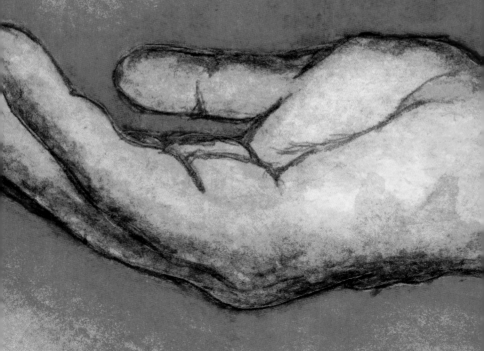

I can give you
love,
but I can't force you to
receive it.

*Puedo darte amor, pero no puedo
forzarte a recibirlo.*

I can teach you to
share,
but I can't stop
you from being
selfish.

*Puedo enseñarte a compartir, pero no
puedo evitar que seas egoísta.*

I can teach you to **respect,** but I can't make you be **respected.**

Puedo enseñarte a respetar, pero no puedo forzarte a ser digno.

I can
counsel you
about your
friends,

Puedo aconsejarte acerca de tus amigos,
pero no puedo escogerlos por ti.

but I can't **choose**
them for you.

I can
teach you
everything you need to
know about your body,

• • •

*Puedo enseñarte todo lo que hay que
saber acerca de tu cuerpo,*

but I can't
make you act
responsibly.

• • •

*pero no puedo hacerte actuar
responsablemente.*

I can
talk
to you about drinking,
but I can't say
"no" or "just one"
for you.

*Puedo hablarte acerca de la bebida, pero no
puedo decir "no" o "solo una" por ti.*

I can **warn** you about drugs, but I can't **stop** you from using them.

Puedo advertirte acerca de las drogas, pero no puedo prevenir que las uses.

I can talk to you about having important **goals,** but I can't **achieve** them for you.

Puedo hablarte de metas importantes, pero no puedo alcanzarlas por ti.

I can teach you about **charity,** but I can't make you be **generous.**

Puedo enseñarte lo que es la bondad,
pero no puedo forzarte a ser generoso.

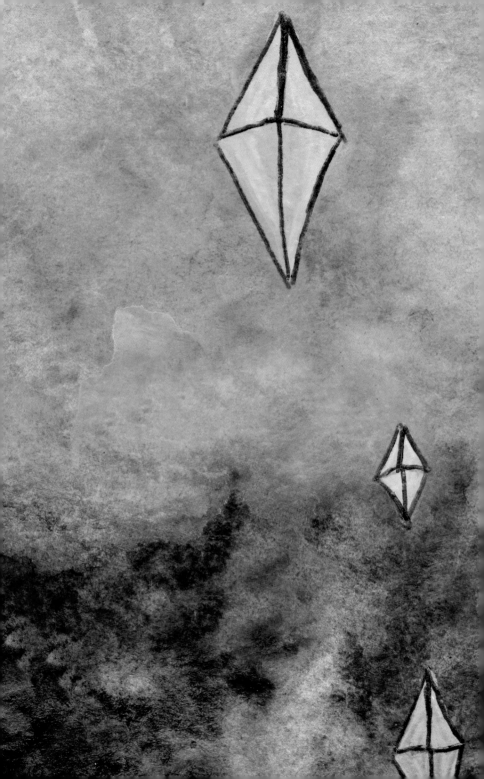

I can
talk to you
about how to live life, but
I won't be at your side
forever.

Puedo hablarte de cómo vivir, pero no estaré a tu lado por siempre.

When everything is **said** and **done,**

Al final de cuentas: cada uno decide por sí mismo y cómo va a llevar su vida.

everybody
decides for him or herself how they will
live their
life.

I **love** you,
I **accept** you,

and I hope with all my

heart

that you make the right decisions.

Te quiero, te acepto y espero con todo mi corazón que decidas lo mejor.

ABOUT THE AUTHOR:
PATRICK ATKINSON

Patrick John Atkinson was raised in Bismarck, North Dakota and attended Minnesota State University–Moorhead. After graduation in 1981, Patrick turned down lucrative corporate job offers to work with runaways, prostitutes, and gang members in New York City's Hell's Kitchen. Two years later, Patrick moved to Central America where he began a twenty-five-year international career in war-zone reconciliation and post-war reconstruction. He has been knighted, is the recipient of numerous human rights awards (including the Guatemalan Congressional Medal) and is the subject of the biogra-. phy, The Dream Maker, by Monica Hannan. Patrick is most proud of having been named Father of the Year by his son, Ernesto, this book's illustrator. He is the founder and executive director of the Institute for Trafficked, Exploited & Missing Persons (ITEMP). He is the author / co-author of six books, and is simultaneously working on books seven, eight, and nine. When not being shot at, knifed, caught in car-bombings, or traveling worldwide advocating on behalf of abused, abandoned, or human-trafficking victims, Patrick resides in Bismarck, North Dakota, in Guatemala, Central America, and at Hippo Wallow Pond; his family home outside of Minneapolis, Minnesota.

AtkinsonCenter.org
ITEMP.org

ABOUT THE ILLUSTRATOR:
ERNESTO ATKINSON

Ernesto "Neto" Atkinson was born and raised in Antigua, Guatemala. Even as a young boy, Ernesto expressed a great interest in art, and over the years his artistic influences grew with tremendous passion. After graduating from El Gran Moyas High School in 1999, Ernesto traveled the world where he explored the arts and understanding of the human existence. He attended North Dakota State University where he began an architectural career but later focused more on the arts. He graduated in 2007 with a degree in visual arts. He earned his Masters in Art Therapy from the School of the Art Institute of Chicago, and is both a professional artist and practicing Licensed Professional Counselor. His first book, 'Integration Art', in which he will present his innovative client centered, seven-step therapeutic process, is expected out soon. He has been called "an artist who truly sees art as an active agent of change"; his work represents a contemporary movement which observes his experiences with everyday life, political and religious concepts, and philosophies. Ernesto's art is a mix of different media that represents the different faces and dissimilarities of society with her incomparable and multiple textures and colors. Ernesto resides with his family in Milwaukee, Wisconsin, works nationally, and displays his art online and through galleries worldwide.

AlivioIntegral.com
Integration-Healing.com

Proceeds from the worldwide sales of *The Powerful You / Message for My Child* are donated to care for and educate the 5,000+ orphaned children and abandoned women helped through The Atkinson Center (www.AtkinsonCenter.org) and associated programs.

YOU are needed by people, animals, and our world. Please choose any charity that interests you and get involved.

The Atkinson Center
Promoting Peace through
Development, Education, and Leadership